MILITARY
HELICOPTERS

PICTURE LIBRARY
MILITARY
HELICOPTERS

C.J. Norman

Franklin Watts

London   New York   Sydney   Toronto

First published in Great Britain
   1986 by
Franklin Watts Ltd
12a Golden Square
London W1R 4BA

First published in the USA by
Franklin Watts Inc
387 Park Avenue South
New York
N.Y. 10016

First published in Australia by
Franklin Watts
14 Mars Road
Lane Cove
2066 NSW

UK ISBN: 0 86313 3541
US ISBN: 0-531-10090-1
Library of Congress Catalog Card
Number 85-51454

Printed in Italy
by Tipolitografia G. Canale & C. S.p.A. - Turin

Designed by
Barrett & Willard

Photographs by
Aerospatiale
Agusta Group
N.S. Barrett Collection
Bell Helicopter Textron
Boeing Vertol Company
British Aerospace
McDonnell Douglas Helicopter Co
UK Land Forces HQ
US Army
US Navy
Westland Helicopters
S. Willard

Illustration by
Janos Marffy/Jillian Burgess Artists

Technical Consultant
Bernard Fitzsimons

Series Editor
N.S. Barrett

Contents

Introduction

Helicopters play an important part in modern warfare. Various types of helicopters are used by both sea and land forces.

Military helicopters are used at sea for hunting and destroying submarines and for attacking enemy ships. On land, they carry troops and supplies and also serve as reconnaissance and fighting craft in support of ground forces.

△ A Sea King helicopter lands on the flight deck of a destroyer. Navy helicopters play an important role in anti-submarine warfare.

Helicopters need very little space for taking off and landing. They can operate from the decks of small warships or even merchant ships.

On land, helicopters can come down on rough or uneven ground. Or they can hover just above the ground to land troops or supplies.

Although helicopters are slow compared with planes, they make up for this with their great maneuverability.

△ A Lynx helicopter firing an anti-tank missile. The army uses helicopters to attack armored vehicles and supply columns.

The attack helicopter

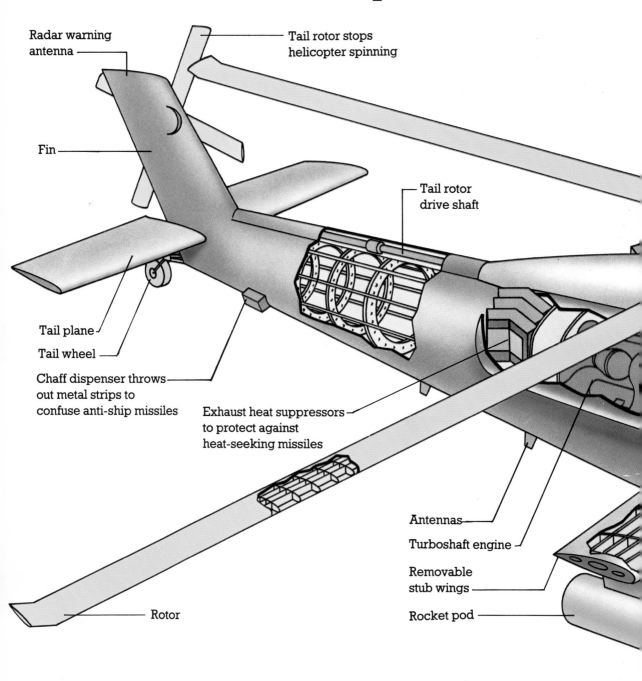

Radar warning antenna

Tail rotor stops helicopter spinning

Fin

Tail rotor drive shaft

Tail plane

Tail wheel

Chaff dispenser throws out metal strips to confuse anti-ship missiles

Exhaust heat suppressors to protect against heat-seeking missiles

Antennas

Turboshaft engine

Removable stub wings

Rotor

Rocket pod

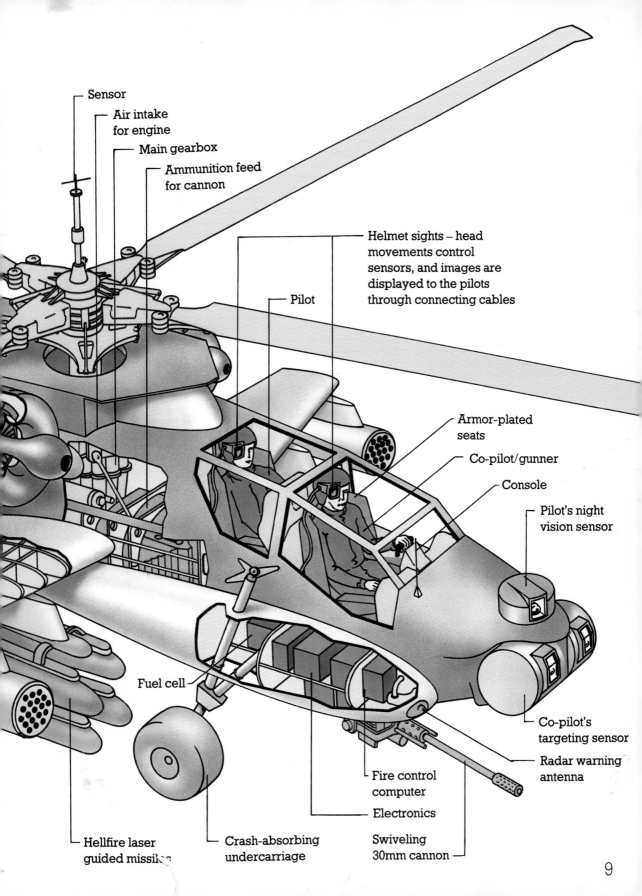

Sensor

Air intake
for engine

Main gearbox

Ammunition feed
for cannon

Helmet sights – head
movements control
sensors, and images are
displayed to the pilots
through connecting cables

Pilot

Armor-plated
seats

Co-pilot/gunner

Console

Pilot's night
vision sensor

Fuel cell

Co-pilot's
targeting sensor

Radar warning
antenna

Fire control
computer

Electronics

Hellfire laser
guided missiles

Crash-absorbing
undercarriage

Swiveling
30mm cannon

Utility helicopters

Some helicopters are designed to carry out a number of light tasks. These general purpose, or utility, craft are used for low-level observation – of their own side's movements as well as the enemy's.

They are also used for transport of personnel or light equipment. Some utility helicopters may be armed with machine guns or even with missiles.

△ The Huey has been used by Western forces as a general purpose helicopter for more than twenty years.

▷ An Agusta A 109A (above), with three other Agustas on the ground. The A 109A is armed with missiles. The Gazelle (below) is fast and light and is often used for training.

Fighting helicopters

Some utility helicopters can be adapted for use as fighting craft. Missiles are attached to the helicopter, usually at the sides, and firing equipment is fitted.

Special versions of utility helicopters have been built for use as fighting machines. The main difference is the amount of electronic equipment required by attack helicopters.

△ The Lynx is a utility helicopter that may be armed for anti-tank warfare. This one is firing a Hellfire missile.

▷ The Defender is an advanced version of the Hughes Model 500M utility helicopter specially designed for anti-tank warfare. It is equipped with a missile system and sensors for detecting vehicles on the ground.

The latest fighting helicopters are specially designed for attack. They are used to hunt and destroy enemy tanks and helicopters. They have a crew of two, with the pilot seated behind the gunner.

These craft have heavy armor plating underneath to protect them from ground attack. They also have equipment to confuse enemy missile systems.

▽ The Apache, an attack helicopter, is equipped with guided missiles and anti-tank rockets. It came into operation in the early 1980s to replace the HueyCobra.

△ The front view (left) and the cockpit (right) of a Mangusta, or A 129, an attack helicopter that came into service in the mid-1980s. The pilot sits behind the co-pilot, who fires the weapons and navigates.

◁ The Lynx 3 is an anti-tank helicopter. The pilot and co-pilot sit next to each other.

Transport helicopters

Transport helicopters carry troops and supplies to the field of battle. They are also used to supply or rescue troops behind enemy lines. They may be equipped as ambulances to carry wounded troops to hospital.

Troops and supplies may be set down by helicopter or they may be parachuted to the ground.

△ The inside of a Chinook. The large opening is at the back, and large loads or vehicles may be winched into place. Seats for troops may be folded up into the sides when not in use. Chinooks can carry more than 40 troops.

▷ Paratroopers wait to make their parachute jumps through a hatch in the floor.

▽ Parachute jumps from helicopters may also be made from the rear.

△ A field gun carried underneath a Chinook transport helicopter. Heavy or extra loads may be carried in this way.

◁ A Chinook hovers while ground crew hook up a vehicle to its lifting gear.

Helicopters fly regular missions to keep invasion forces supplied with equipment, ammunition and rations. They operate across water and territory that cannot be reached by other means.

The larger transport helicopters, such as the Chinook, can carry jeeps, field guns or even heavy trucks. The heavier loads are suspended underneath the body of the helicopter.

▽ The cockpit of a Puma. Transport helicopters have two pilots who sit next to each other.

▷ A Puma flies off after setting down troops during a winter exercise in northern Europe.

Helicopters can work in extreme weather conditions. They take supplies and troops to jungle clearings or to desert or snow-covered areas, where they cannot be moved by road.

In freezing weather, special heating elements or other methods are used to keep the rotor blades free from ice.

Navy helicopters

Most warships carry at least one or two helicopters. The chief role of navy helicopters is to search for and destroy enemy helicopters, warships and submarines.

Helicopters use sonar, a method for detecting submarines by means of sound echoes. They can also use radar to spot danger from distant enemy ships, planes or missiles.

△ An aircraft handling officer watches a Sea King anti-submarine helicopter take off from the deck of an assault ship.

△ The Seahawk, an anti-submarine helicopter, is the navy version of the army Blackhawk.

◁ A crewman attaches a cable to a Seahawk. This is a special device for landing safely in rough weather. Like most navy helicopters, Seahawks perform a range of duties, such as carrying supplies and personnel to other ships or evacuating casualties.

△ A Lynx deploying a device known as MAD, or Magnetic Anomaly Detector. This detects the presence of submarines by a magnetic effect.

◁ A Sea King using a dipping sonar device, for detecting submarines by sound.

▷ A Lynx launching a homing torpedo.

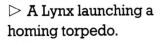

Helicopters fire all kinds of missiles. They use torpedoes to attack submarines. Some helicopters can carry heavy long-range missiles, such as the Exocet, for use against large warships. Smaller missiles have been specially designed for use with light helicopters.

Some navy helicopters are used for transporting men and supplies between ships. They also stand by for emergencies and rescue anyone in trouble in the sea.

△ A Super Puma carrying Exocets, very powerful long-range missiles. These are capable of destroying large warships.

▷ A Lynx firing a Sea Skua, a sea-skimming, short-range missile used against small ships and fast patrol craft.

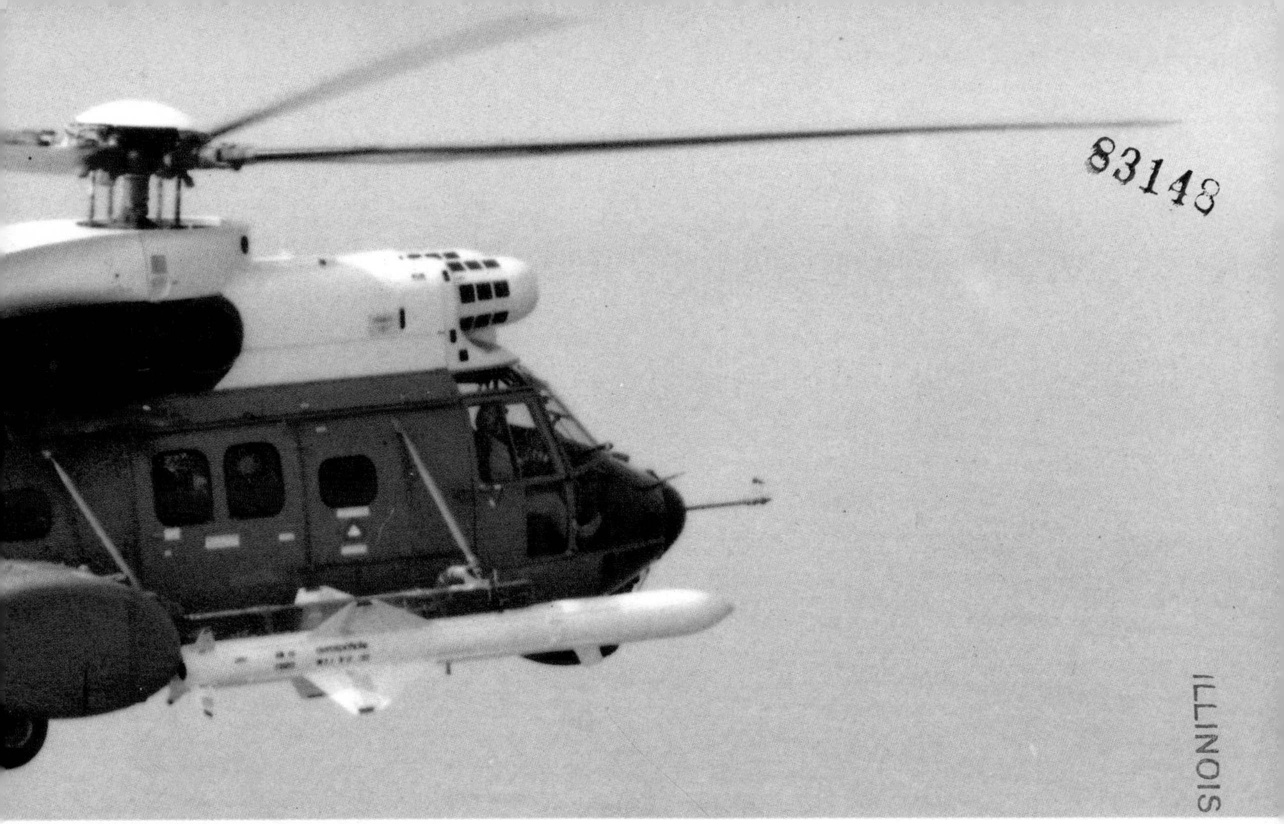

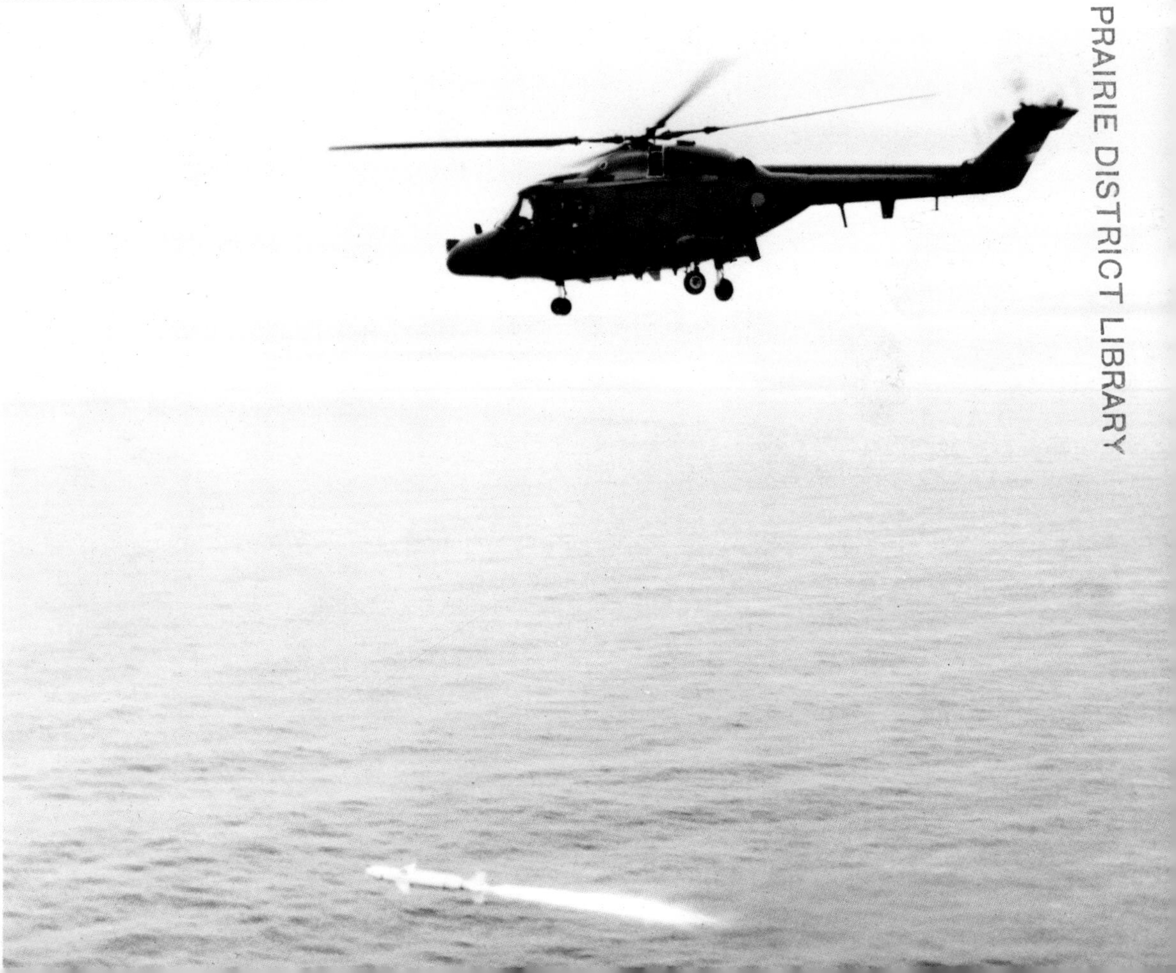

The story of combat helicopters

The Hoverfly

The first helicopter built for military service was the Sikorsky R-4, or Hoverfly, which made its maiden flight in 1942 in the United States. More than 400 of these helicopters were built. They were used mainly for transport and rescue operations by the British and US forces near the end of World War II.

△ A Hoverfly in operation on a World War II aircraft carrier.

Rescue and assault

It was not until the Korean War, in the early 1950s, that the importance of helicopters in warfare became established. One of their chief uses was as aerial ambulances. They were also used for communications, reconnaissance and for the transportation of supplies to areas that were impossible to reach by other means. It was also the first attempt to use helicopters to fly in marines during assault operations.

Arming helicopters

In the 1950s, to provide cover against enemy ground fire, troops fired rifles and sub-machine guns from the open doors of helicopters. Later, special armament systems were developed that could be easily fitted into a helicopter. These were a combination of machine guns, cannon and rockets fixed on either side of the fuselage. Machine guns were also mounted on the doors.

The "helicopter war"

The war in Vietnam, which lasted from 1957 to 1975, was sometimes called the "helicopter war." For the first time, helicopters played a major part in the fighting. Armament systems were developed for both defensive and offensive roles.

It has been estimated that 90

△ The Huey was the chief US helicopter in the Vietnam war.

out of every 100 US casualties were evacuated from Vietnam combat areas by helicopter. The Huey, the chief troop-carrying helicopter, could also be fitted out as an aerial ambulance or as an armed escort craft. Chinooks were used for carrying guns, ammunition and other supplies. They could hold more than 10 tons of equipment or take 30 to 40 combat troops. The even larger Sikorsky Skycranes could carry big howitzers or take 45 troops. They were sometimes equipped as field hospitals.

The first helicopter to be designed purely for fighting, as a "gunship," was the HueyCobra, which came into service in 1967.

△ The HueyCobra was the first of the specially designed gunships.

Helicopters at sea

Helicopters began to operate from smaller ships in the 1960s, as well as from aircraft carriers. Since then, the chief role of naval helicopters has been in anti-submarine warfare and air-sea rescue.

△ The British Navy version of the Lynx, the first helicopter to sink a ship – in the Falklands War of 1982.

Latest advances

In recent years advances have included more powerful engines including jet engines. Designers are constantly making improvements in performance and safety. Attempts to build a helicopter that converts into a plane after take off are still in the experimental stage.

△ An artist's impression of the EH101, a helicopter of the late 1980s.

Facts and records

△ The Mi-26, or Halo, the world's largest military helicopter.

Largest

The world's largest military helicopter is the Soviet Mi-26, known in the West as the Halo. It weighs 56 tons and is nearly 111 ft (34 m) long. It can carry about 100 troops and crew. A larger Soviet helicopter, the Mi-12, was built, but never went into production.

△ The Sea Stallion, the largest helicopter in the West.

Fastest

The speed record for helicopters was set by the Mi-24, known as the Hind. It reached a speed of 229 mph (368 km/h) on a special record attempt in 1978.

△ The fastest helicopter, the Mi-24, or Hind.

Tilt-rotor craft

Experiments have been going on for many years to produce a craft with the lift of a helicopter and the speed and range of a plane. The most advanced of these craft is the Bell XV-15, which has rotors that tilt forward and serve as propellers during flight. A number of test craft, or proto-types, of these have been built.

△ The Bell XV-15 tilt rotor craft.

Glossary

Cannon
The main guns on a helicopter. They fire shells.

Chaff
Strips of metal foil thrown out by helicopters to confuse enemy missiles, whose radar cannot distinguish them from the helicopter.

Gunship
A helicopter heavily armed with guns and missiles.

Heat-seeking missiles
Missiles that home in on the engine heat of aircraft. Some helicopters have suppressors to disperse the heat so that it does not present such an obvious target for the missiles.

Homing torpedo
A torpedo that homes in on the sound of a ship's or submarine's engines.

Paratroopers
Troops that parachute out of aircraft.

Radar
A system used for detecting targets by means of special radio waves.

Reconnaissance
Reconnaissance helicopters make a survey of enemy positions or movements.

Rotors
Rotors spin around to propel the helicopter. They have a number of blades and are driven by the engines.

Sensors
Detecting devices that provide the crew and the computer system with necessary information.

Sonar
A method that uses sound waves underwater to detect targets.

Tilt rotor
A rotor that can be tilted to act as an airplane propeller in flight. Tilt rotor craft are still in the experimental stage.

Utility helicopter
A helicopter that may be fitted out for several different purposes, such as transport or rescue work, communications, reconnaissance or fighting.

Index